From Infinity To Infinity

Vol. 2

Dijon Bowden

Dijon Bowden
www.dijonbowden.com

ISBN: 978-1-7352328-3-6

Printed in the United States of America
First Printing, 2021

Editing: Tell Tell Poetry | www.telltellpoetry.com
Interior Design: Cover&Layout | www.coverandlayout.com
Cover Design: Dijon Bowden | www.dijonbowden.com

DEDICATION

For Syd

I found the will to be my Self
in your reflection

Sat Nam

CONTENTS

III

Fractalized Unity

When I say I,
I mean you.

When I say you,
I mean me.

When either is mentioned,
I reference we.

There is only one of us here.

The Source and its reflections
meditate to become clear,
then embrace illumined golden perception.

ILLUMINATED ESSENCE

Pulling the poison from my mind,
exposing the projections that keep me seeing
through bats' eyes.

Illuminating the cosmic essence of the sublime
with devotion to the formless being beyond time—

clarifying esoteric wisdom in rhyme,
celebrating sacred

S P A C E

between lines.

Love Is

Love is real.
Love is true.

Love is whatever spirit tells you to do.

Love is patient.
Love is kind.

Love is diving into the ocean of your heart
and climbing out of the quicksand of your mind.

Love is me.
Love is you.

Love lets you die,
so you can start anew.

PEACEFUL PANDA

You control the depth.
You control the speed.
You decide when you experience peace.

Life can be simple.
Life can be fun
when you surrender   to   ease
life has just begun.

Crimson Chrysalis

Spirit places its lips on my soul
to perform lightning streaked mouth to mouth.

The pressure crushes me from the inside out.

My brittle body writhes
with the shock of an electric chair
as it breathes in
thunderstruck air.

Burnt sienna voltage illuminates my skin,
exposing all that's within.

Translucence reveals both virtue and sin.

Spring Forward

Earth spins on its axis
as seasons change.

Winter's incubation period is thawing out—

mental patterns of sloth and doubt
are invited to slink away
like condensation on the outside
of a tall glass of lemonade.

What will this new chapter bring?

What song will these auspicious birds sing

on these cool sunny days leading into spring?

Back to West Africa

I return to the ancient African roots
of my family tree
to unchain tortured souls,
so they can finally be free.

Laying out my lineage
for all beings to see,
following our circular ascent
from Slavery to Divinity.

With loving presence we
go forth with glee,
joyfully inhabiting
the world we're consciously creating.

MUSHIN

I am ready to embrace the next season of my life.

I am molded clay in a kiln,
caressed by the hands of the divine
as Prana is sent through my breath
up the lumbar, thoracic, and cervical chambers of my spine.

The final coat of glaze is placed upon me,
as I begin my days of exploration—
my journey halted before it has even begun.

Father wind blows me off my center,
I crumble to the ground,
smashed and splintered.

The master potter picks me up gently
as I bloom in multiple hues
like the flowers on the tree from a Lantana seed.

Transforming teaches me the ancient art of Kintsugi,
filling my cracks with watermelon wonder and golden alchemy.

Dijon Bowden

Grandmother's Vine

Parallel lines intertwine
for an entire lifetime,

living rooted
in the heart,
backed by the service
of a disciplined mind.

Climbing Grandmother's vine
to the unified divine,
we shine

outside the confines
of Space
and Time.

PERFECT PEACE

My greatest desire is to know peace,
feeling the apricot glow of the sun
while the wind tickles my body
from my crown to my feet.

My roots run deep like ancient redwood trees
through the portal at the core of the Earth
to cosmic galaxies.

I inspire with magical frequencies from my leaves,
as I freely offer newly ripened fruit from my avocado tree.

This harvest bountifully feeds
my kin, my friends, and my remembrance of singularity.

Ice-olation

The human in me is lonely.

How perfect do I have to be
to feel part of a family that accepts me?

I know the truth
is that I must learn to accept myself,
to love all my parts
and see each day as a new start,

but some days I feel so blue,
and the only thing I want to hold is you.

Is that type of love a corrosion of mind,
one that keeps creating separation
time after time?

I'm driven to turn within
and altar my breath,
because no one but me can save me,
not even beloved death.

Eternal Sunshine

Eternity is exquisite with you.
Your sunflower soul sparkles with truth.
The luminous energy exuding from your being
is joyous, playful, inviting, and freeing.

Your multi-dimensional beauty is an inspiring reflection,
reminding me that rising in love requires authenticity,
not perfection.

Creating with you is easeful and light.
Our connection illuminates the path to heavenly heights.

AWESTRUCK

Learn to be in awe of the pain

one thousand miles above sea level,

looking from the

S O U R C E

of the rain.

QUEEN OF THE JUNGLE

Love is a lion.
The gate to her chamber is a mirage.

Her womb births celestial beings,
fractalized expressions of geometrical seedlings.

The flower of life divides from one to two
so that duality's contrast can reveal the true you.

PROGRESS

Simplicity is wisdom.
Presence is truth.
I'm grateful to be integrating
the intense lessons of youth.

My spirit still spry,
although less tempestuous and glib,
the shifting of seasons
invites in new ways to live.

Regal Roots

Sparks ignite a fire within my ribcage.
The vibes run up my smokestack sternum.

Awake and alive is the malachite mind state.

We roll our intentions up,

let go,

and burn 'em.

Feeling deeply,
we know what is to ensue.

My ancestors whisper their secrets,
speaking stories in Bantu.

We relax and remember our West African home,
laughing because we know we'll return to the throne.

RADICAL REFLECTIONS

Is your partner to blame
when the dance of relating drives you insane?

Is the notion that your emotions
are yours to have and to hold ring true
as you process fiery red and icy blue?

Is your lover there to always be by your side,
or do they reflect parts of you that you're trying to hide?

This one thing I know to be true:
the other you feel so attached to is you,

a mirror that maps the way through the maze
into full awakening and out of slumbering haze.

Lose your mind to gain your soul.
Open your heart and release control.
Live in service to fly free and become whole.

A CORNUCOPIA OF KARMA

Creativity is a choice,
it's deciding to speak with God's voice,
it's releasing

attachment to the noise—

it's beginning at the end
with spiritual allies and
venomous friends,
no piece turned away,
a cornucopia of karma
and it all can stay.

For I am the light
that shines through the darkness,
and I am also the shadow
you must learn to harness—

Integrated
Happy
Free

When I look into your eyes,
I see me.

21

I am so grateful

I've learned
to simply *be*.

Clear Eyes

With a full heart, I'll share what's been unlocked for me:
the keys to living joyfully
are presence, gratitude, and simplicity.

Nature is God.

From her womb we were birthed,
harmony achieved by tuning into her
as we build a new Earth.

Out of density and darkness

to levity and truth.
We rewrite the history of humanity's youth.

A new age of connection and peace
unfolds as ego-driven actions cease.

Sacred Serenity

Patience has nothing to do with time.
There is no such thing as time.

Patience is the pressure you put on the present
to be what you want it to be at that precise moment.

Patience isn't necessary if you practice presence.

There is always a precious gift in the present to be appreciated.

Practice presence patiently.

Feral Eyes

When you're lost,
how is it you become found?
When you're spun out,
what practices do you use to ground?

Freedom begins
the moment you realize
there is no end.

Then you see
honeysuckle and jasmine
twisting gingerly

in the wind.

Hummingbirds float
before your feral eyes,
the moon cactuses' dance
reveals a magnificent surprise.

Click your heels three times
to wake up from the lies.

BOUNDLESS

25

Logic has limits,
        but love is infinite.

II

Melodic Temptation

Enveloping tones and vibratory scales
transmit nostalgia
and kaleidoscopic tales
of love, lust, redemption, and sin,

a potent concoction
for an epic saga to begin:

melodic stories told
of days crimson and gold,

wisdom regained
by learning to find joy
in pain.

Tickling 88 ebony and ivory keys
is a magical and glorious thing,
but the soul is regained
when the unvoiced heart is allowed to sing.

ME ME ME

My ego causes more problems than me know,
but the sequel blooms more fruit than the prequel—

Release
Flow—

overstand the nature of good and evil,
time to create new paradigms to deprogram the people.

Yellow Brick Road

Finding the courage to live your dream
can prove harder than it seems.

You'd think it would be easy to choose to be free,
after all, don't we want to live happily?

So why is it that we settle for what we can see,
even though we know we're not living optimally?

The soul waits patiently for us to surrender to its call.

Defensiveness attracts attacks.
Pride comes before the fall,

the great fall into the depths of the infinite sea
of love, peace, joy, and blessed unity.

No matter where you have wandered along the winding road,
you're one turn away from returning to the path back home.

SPACIOUS AND FREE

I feel unattached,

s p a c i o u s,

and   free,

available to life
and infinite possibility.

No need to hold on,
I trust in the flow.

It's never felt so good
to surrender

and let go.

Trinity

The spirit conceives;
the mind creates what it believes;
the body experiences.

Joy is sacred.
Sex is life.
Embrace pleasure-filled presence without strife.

You don't need a reason to do anything,
just be the cause.
Take a pause,

now choose who you want to be.

Connect with your soul.
Stand in your truth.
Release control;
let love make you whole.

Expressing Blessings

The joy of being human
is the beauty of choice,
limitless possibilities
to express your Self's voice.

Every decision you make
makes a statement about you;
choose wisely
and remember this ultimate truth:

there is no hell,
no punishment for a target missed,

only rejecting or embracing
everlasting joy and bliss.

UNI-VERSE

Do it when you're tired.
Do it when you're scared.
Do it when you're the only one there.

Do it cause you can.
Do it to be free.
Do it just because—

do it for me.

Do it for him.
Do it for her.
Do it to begin again.

Do it to be sure.

Do it cause it's right.
Do it cause it's wrong—

no matter how you sing,
there's only one song.

BEING TRUST

Pause,
rest easy,
you are protected.

Lay down your defenses,
and stay connected.

Slow down,
breathe deep,
remember the truth—

give thanks
for Earth under your feet—
embody the real you.

Stay the Course

Have faith, little one.
Your greatest triumph is yet to come.

Hold steady in your vision of me.
Your perseverance will most assuredly set you free.

Your heart is the key that opens all doors;
trust in your Self and you will suffer no more.

Surrender to the Void

Rest,
be easy,
release craving, force, and greed.

Rest,
be easy,
you already have everything you need.

Rest,
be easy,
it's okay to slow down.

Surrender to the void,
and lay your burdens down.

INNER G

Open your heart,
and relax your mind
for truth is treasure buried within you.

Release control,
and follow your soul
for you are not the stories you've lived through.

All is well,
and you will excel
when you release the flow of the serpent.

You hold the key
to eternity
when you embrace presence in the present.

SENSUAL SEDUCTION

What if my primary objective in writing is pleasure?
What if EYE construct every sonnet
with the intent to slowly savor every sentence?

Each word is a morsel of the delicacy of my mind's expression,
inviting you to taste the texture of the words as they're formed
in your mouth as you read them aloud.

Scintillating stimulation of the senses—stroking your septum,
the air slides along your tongue, tickling the roof of your mouth
like an effervescent spritzer sprinkling drops of joy on your soul.

KNOW YOURSELF

What others think about you is a reflection of them.
How you respond is a reflection of you.
When you are attacked and feel fear,
do you still believe love is the ultimate Truth?

If so, you are one with the sea,
beyond duality,
pain is part of everyone's story,
but it too can set you free.

Every trauma can awaken you
to hear the voice of your soul;

attacks point out cracks
you need to face to become whole.

Terms of Engagement

The beauty of becoming
is such a wondrous sight.
If you're lost in the dark,
look within to find your light.

Manifest your preference,
move with power, not deference.

You are the entirety of existence.

In your heart, you know this as law,
your awakening achieved by persistence;
doubting yourself is your only flaw.

Fear attracts things to you;
wanting them pushes them away.

The world is a big playground;
you just have to learn the rules to play.

Tomorrow Always Knows

Truth is a vibration.
You know when something rings true.
Death is an illusion.
It's simply transformation into another form of you.

Heaven is always here,
available in the eternal *now*.

The cosmic entrance appears
when you open the eye between your brows.

ATLANTIAN DREAMS

Release late nights in front of a screen.
Netflix binging turns into woefully wasting your seed.
The loveless images you see
are smokescreens for energy-sucking entities.

Invest in your vitality by harvesting sleep.
Travel through surreal realms of magenta, purple, and green.

Open your heart and mind to receive
the intergalactic transmissions of your Pleiadean star family.

OPEN DOOR

Thank you for sharing
your wounds and your pain.
Your vulnerability
helps me feel safe and feel sane.

I love you
for creating this space for intimacy.
I love you
because in you I see me.

It's important to know
that we're never alone,
perfect reflections of expanding perspectives
walking hand in hand home.

DIVINE UNION

Enraptured by the symphony of nature's song,
crickets sweetly serenade
while the tree frogs sing along.

Stars illuminate the cosmos,
showing me what I felt
as the lines between me and the external world melt.

The divine mind has granted me access
to a new dimension,
same coordinates,
different axis.

In this place things are not what they seem,
banality turns to beauty,
fulfilling my heart's dream.

Fuchsia Frenzy

Do you long to be free, beloved?
Are you tired of the frantic tempo?
Slow down and breath deep, beloved.
It's really all quite simple.

Heaven is found in the present moment.
Ascension is gifted by grace.
Does that explanation of the universe
bring a smile to your face?

I know you like to make it hard
and distract yourself with drama and struggle,
but can you open to the healing of your scars
by receiving vibrations strong and subtle?

FIRM FOUNDATION

Two revolutions around the sun,
and we're still hitched at the hip,
two satellites dancing through candy colored cosmic mist.

A tripwire is triggered,
and I burn up with my Vata.
She sways in the breeze
cooling me with her waters.

Regaining form, I rise from sacred dust.
This is the first connection I know built from peace,
not lust.

SACRED ORGASMIC LIVING

I want to touch you
where clever meets truth,
where wisdom meets youth,
making one out of two.

I want to feel you
and swallow your tongue,
your fragrance my dinner;
my lips make you come.

I want to know you
mind, body, and soul.
Your laughter sparks sunflowers.
With you I feel whole.

The Cosmic Ocean

The clock nears midnight,
and I'm reunited with old friends,
grateful for the opportunity to begin again.

Rivers break into differentiated streams
while heaven shines down ultraviolet light beams.

Against the currents the waters flow
until they surrender and

let go—

once they do,
they float downstream,
united in the ocean
in a galactic dream.

III

Seeds of Love

Plant seeds of love in her heart,
and let them bloom.

Don't rush to harvest them too soon.

The bounty is for her to enjoy
under the vibrations of the Scarlett Moon.

Let her choose to share the overflow
however she chooses to.

Keep your center,
and focus on you.
Continue communing with God,
and see it all the way through.

STABLE ROOTS

I choose a solid foundation

over instant gratification,

honoring the totality
within me.

I preserve my seed
and embrace your bleed
to create a grounded family tree.

True Self

Striking a balance between
self-aware and self-involved,

standing on the edge of the precipice,
but I won't fall.

I'm learning to fall to my knees
to stand tall,

to face what scares me most
inside my own walls.

GROUND INTO TRUTH

Your soul cries red
as your heart bleeds blue.
Tears trickle down your face
once the truth breaks through.

You climb towards a field of baby sunflowers
who long for their father, the Sun, to hold them.

As you approach,
their saccharine scent envelops your aura,
transporting you into timelessness.

The sky is gray;
the moon is too.
Your reflection in the stream

B I R T H S

a miracle.

The brook speaks up
as the light shines through.

59

She says,
>Dear one,
>I am God,
>and you are too.

Sacramento Sojourn

We went on a mission for condoms, croissants, and pizza—

you warned me not to stuff myself on bread and dough,
to save my appetite and taste your radiant glow.

The fluidity and play of our second meeting
showed our connection was more than fleeting.

Our energies more fluid, lively, and light,
our sweetest moment came after making love one night.

I watched *Suits* while you traversed the depths of her waves,
our hands interlinked as the peace we rested in grew
and, when you thought I had fallen asleep,
you whispered in my ear,

I like you.

Dijon Bowden

Princess Pachamama

The sacred waters in the Peruvian valley suit you well.

The hue of your olive skin speaks
of the union with spirit within.

I wonder what white river rapids whisper to your soul
as you let Source take the wheel and relinquish control.

You model devotion with grace and ease,
despite thousands of miles between us,
we meet in my ajna each morning on my knees.

Upon arising, I read your poetry as a reminder to be,
becoming the next indigo version of me.

Divinity dwells in every reflection,
and I see it everywhere when I am rooted in Truth,

but my heart feels most inspired when
I imagine her face to look like you.

Marcus Garvey and Mental Slavery

Decolonize your mind
to have clear perception;

otherwise they'll use your own vision
as their greatest weapon.

Inner Sanctum

Connection is essential for us to feel sane
and yet enmeshment causes acute, all-consuming pain.

Life isn't worth living
without your heart being caressed.

You need to be touched on your soul, skin, and chest.

To maintain balance in the relational dance,
don't leave the attunement of your vibration to chance—

practice daily devotion on the path to self-mastery,
knowing that to truly connect with another,
you must sustain Self-sovereignty.

Bitter Fruit

Mirrored reflections reveal to me
that my diet contains the bitter fruits of fantasy.

The remedy to live life with ease
is to clear the samskaras
and embrace absolute reality;

conscious control of the breath through

Pranayama

makes your mind sattvic
and evaporates life's drama.

When intuition is received,
you can decipher
the secrets of the trees
and the language of the breeze—
all whispering,

You've always been free.

Astringent Passage

Bitter berries taste better
when you realEYEs
every doorway ultimately opens into

Healing—

life is a journey through
Earth, Water, Fire, Air, and Ether
to induce dynamic

Feeling.

Solar Flares

Dancing in the radiance of her herbaceous grace,
being blessed by the joy on her face
allows contemplation
as a pure sensation
of a world beyond reason and relativity

to the absolute truth
where eternal youth calls us
with the promise of immunity.

Immortality obtained
and unshakeable vitality regained
by mixing scarlet surrender
with dandelion devotion.

SANTA MARIA

Laced with the Goddess Code
in the belly of *Cafe Sunflower*,
I receive the secret
to unlimited power.

Release dense frequencies that bring down the vibe.
Count your blessings,
and celebrate life with tribe.

Cultivate creative energy
by prioritizing inner peace.

Greater than paper
or external wealth
is the complete realization
and embodiment of your divine, immortal Self.

Cooling Rain

Feeling into the trigger,
witnessing the pain,
plotting an escape,
cleansed by cooling rains,

breath washes away fear,
as the tide splashes upon the shore.

I accept what's here *now*
and release the need for more.

This moment is all there is,
so I surrender to the flow.
I breathe into the wound—
I exhale and let go.

Icy Flames

I burned a heart with icy flames;
confusion and loneliness remain.

Sun-scorched sunflowers
wilt from one-hundred-degree heat,
thirsting for water at the root,
for sweet relief.

A divine reflection is pushed away,
so that I can regain the pain

of   uninterrupted   space.

Grace mirrors the imperfections I avoid.
It's clearer to face and embrace
all parts within with poise.

Ida and Pingala

The path to prosperity is simple:
plant seeds in the energy field of the collective
and make deposits into the dimension of unity.

Plant seeds of kindness
in the hearts of all you meet.
Plant seeds of devotion,
honoring all the promises you speak.

Deposit good will
into the hearts of all the beings you touch.
Revel in the thrill
of helping souls become unstuck.

Experience every moment
as deliciously divine.
Coax the serpent
up the masculine and feminine channels
crisscrossing your spine.

Raise the energy
to the tip of your crown,
then hypercharge the body
by bringing the Amrit Vela back down.

Walk the Earth awakened and whole,
a human being completely animated by your sacred soul.

Inseminated by Aloha

Bamboo forests swallowed me whole
in my search for Maui's magic.

I put one foot in front of the other
as my toes sunk into the clay-colored mud.

We crossed a plank of wood
over a rapidly running stream
as we entered a new frontier.

The jagged edges of the rocks
in the riverbed
demanded my presence in every step.

We paused to recenter
and work the breath.

Freshly oxygenated,
we pressed on.

She was wild,
so she moved faster than I did,
graceful and fierce at the same time.

She disappeared around a bend,

and when I came around the corner,
the paths diverged and I wasn't sure
which route she had taken—
my back stiffened and I thought,
maybe it's time to turn back.

There was enough space between us
for fear to slither in.

My inhale shallowed,

and I was lost—

then I caught a glimpse
of her hair

and

kept going,

following her lead.

When I came around the corner,
I found her at the base of an ice-cold swimming hole

filled by the flow of a majestic waterfall.

I exhaled and thought to myself,

                    so this is what it feels like to be free.

Home Cooking

God is the wisdom of redwood trees
and the amber honey of Apis bees.

God is the scent of a jacaranda flower
and the homecooked sweet potatoes you devour.

God is the brisk breeze in your hair
and the puissant Prana within air.

God speaks when you are quiet and alone,
guiding you step by step home.

DIJON BOWDEN

OPULENT OMNIPOTENCE

I am the joy
in a newborn's eyes.
I am the pain
of a child bastardized.

I am the life divine
animating your dreams.
I am the sun setting,
giving way to moonbeams.

I am the ethereal essence
persisting across all lifetimes.
I am the darkness
of the abyss in a tortured mind.

I am everything perceived
within and without.
I am the freedom that exists
once you release all doubt.

When you are lost and desire clarity,
speak my name,
and I will open the door to eternity.

The Symphony of Duality

Overcast skies cry.

A tear runs down the cheek of a cumulus cloud.

But nowhere in nature is there any sorrow—
the weeping of one being
fertilizes soil for tomorrow.

The natural cycles move with levity
because each instrument plays a part
in the symphony of duality.

SECRETS OF THE TREES

Ignorant, earthly extraction makes the sacred heart bleed.
You can never get enough of what you don't need.

The distance between heaven and hell
equals the distance between altruism and greed.

In order to end the atrocities of trafficking and slavery,
your tamasic mind (lost in the senses) needs to be freed.

Ritualize standing in the rays of the sun
and swaying with the trees.
They whisper secrets of eternal vitality.

When you stop doing and simply be,
the great wheel spins,
and you enter the gate of eternity.

When your mind goes beyond time,
you can move through PTSD.

Healing comes by sharing the story
of what broke you, vulnerably.

Your tale of initiation and transcendence
is medicine for the community.

Scorpio Moon

Holiness dwells in darkness
as an invitation to a second sight,
a pathway to inner illumination achieved
by finding peace
in gut-wrenching fright.

There are secrets in the heights
of the Anahata chamber
revealed by honoring
the grace of danger.

It's only when we recognize
the beauty of symbiotic duality
that the veil lifts and
we are finally free.

Grasping For Me

The distance between you
and everything you desire

is the distance between you
and your

Self.

IV

TODAY, I AM REBORN

Yesterday, I felt the death of another version of me.

Free, I begin this new chapter

not knowing where I am being led

but not needing to know either.

The gift is in the present,

the process presenting the way,

the way leading me to my center

which is a direction and not a destination.

As I journey inward, I am bathed in an ultraviolet light beam.

The smudge removed from my soul,

allowing me to see more clearly

like new sight after laser eye surgery.

Only then, with new clarity,

do we RealEYEs how distorted our view of reality had become.

This is why death is so beautiful—

she severs our attachments with a scythe and
awakens spiritual vision.

Now is a new day,

and a deeper life begins.

Eternal Love

Love is everlasting.
It is not this it is not that.
It is full spectrum living,
gray shades, not white and black.

I long to hold you,
to finally feel you near.
This I can wholeheartedly admit:
I love you completely without fear.

Not just your body
and not just your soul,
the totality of you,
your sensuous and illustrious whole.

I embrace the call of passion.
Inside you, I long to be,
two waves crashing together,
creating the entirety of the sea.

KEMET

The Egyptian-blue sky split open
and torrential rains floated down.

A nymph kissed me on my crown,
and I laid my burdens down,
dancing in the sacred scarlet showers to the rhythm of my joy.

I remember the freedom
of not needing to know,
in allowing creativity to grow,
in aligning and tuning into the flow

like *water*
soft, sacred, and free,
roaming from a rushing river to the sensual sapphire sea.

Prismatic Prana

I rise

and

jasmine-scented aromatic air thins
as I ascend.

I rise,
climbing my inner mountain,

breathing consciously
to unleash precious Prana within me.

Wise, ancient trees breathe in my exhale,
as I spy the flight of a prismatic nightingale.

She sings a song of complete liberation,
no longer trapped by identifying with transitory sensations—

Unattached, Present, and Free
Eternally.

Naked and Free

Dancing naked,
invisible
to those unacquainted
with   Joy.

Flying above
recalcitrant noise.

Each sliver of the present
a gracious gift from God.
Breath of fire helps the serpent
to remove ego's façade.

The lotus blooms
at the perfect moment.
Self-love
being
the crucial component.

Self-Worth

When you grovel and beg,
you deny your true wealth.

Riches are ready

to reign upon you
once you
embrace your Self.

Remember where you come from,
and your days of suffering are through.

Everything you need already lives inside you.

An Instrument of Healing

I pray to be a clear vessel for Source,
so I may wield power with integrity
and release force.

I pray to be an instrument of healing,
so I may be free from the mind
and embody feeling.

I pray to heed the call of my soul,
so I choose to release grasping
and remember I am whole.

Turning fully to the Truth,
I dismiss distraction.

I hear the calls of my True Self
and tune out the cries for contraction.

I can distinguish between the voices because
the soul creates peace
while ego demands satisfaction.

Unification

What a powerful gift,
the reflection of a lover.
You can heal yourself
through the lens of the other.

Deep unraveling of stories and wounds
made possible in reverence for the sacred womb.

Conscious sexuality
awakens transformative fire.

Be led by the heart's guidance,
not only carnal desire.

Persian Wine

What a blessing it is
to be a vessel for the divine,
an artisanal clay carafe
for the master winemaker's wine.

Quietly quenching the thirst
of souls searching for sacred sustenance.

Laying down my preferences
for the opportunity to be my soul,

trading thoughts of separation
for remembrance of being whole.

Lotus Blossom

Freedom is yours when you choose it.
There's actually no way to lose it.

The feeling that it's gone is illusion,

remembrance obtained by the fusion of the eternal soul
and the whole of the body;

spirit meets matter,
and from the mud blooms Samadhi.

FORBIDDEN FRUIT

Everyone bows to the truth eventually.
When there's no more lying,
you are set free.

As the observer, you accept what is
because, no matter what,
you'll always live.

You are the essence of every flower.
You are the Thunder

before the showers.

95

In the land before time,
you dreamed
of crystalline Kings and loamy Queens.

The union of the two
births forbidden fruit;
for this to happen
one must become two.

Embracing Emptiness

I rest in the womb of sacred silence,
free from the intrusion of sonic violence,
a cacophony of vibration
fighting for individuality
instead of falling into One mentality
of Peace, Patience, Softness, and Harmony.

Feral fertility lies in the ability
to dissolve into no thing—

tapping into totality
is the gift that embracing emptiness brings.

SOULMATES

Her warm waves pepper my body with kisses
as she shines her lunar love beams onto my crown.

She coos,

> *I envisioned this*
> *to untangle your defenses.*
> *Relax your mind,*
> *and lean into your senses.*

The sand beneath our toes
softens beside the ocean blue.

Vulnerability soothes our woes;
this old love story can begin anew.

SOFTENING

I've been afraid to love you
as if my fear isn't easy enough to see through.

My rose blooms within, and I worry I'll need you.
The veins are still tender, they might just bleed blue,

but my true Self knows the way,
and the white lights lead to

Glory.

A new chapter of a different story,
one where we wake up together in the morning
and stay by each other's side when life gets boring.

MAGNETISM

The sprightly sapphire sun surrounded by candy-colored skies
radiates the same energy flowing from your eyes.

The portals to your soul let the light shine through,
and I long to come Home and stand beside you,

our legs intertwined as we ascend to the throne,
we release fear of abandonment and embrace the unknown.

Vital Attraction

Why worry about being successful?

When you are authentic,
light shines through everything you do,
and your dharma's tools will be magnetically drawn to you.

Siphon and Reservoir

Being Selfless and Self-serving
are the same thing.

Fill your own cup before attempting serving.

Becoming full, you begin to glow;
miraculous healing transpires
in the symbiotic toroidal flow.

RESTORATIVE REFLECTIONS

Stop searching for healing;
you are healing.

You are the love you've been looking for,
though we know looks can be deceiving.

Gratitude and Grace

Thank you for the gift of life you have given me.

I celebrate the majesty of the stars
and the power of the sea.

The kiss of the sun's rays sets my soul ablaze
and ceases contemplation of universal mystery.

Presence awakened by mindless simplicity.

Gratitude overflows with appreciation
for the beauty of *now*;
for I remember I am creating this creation.

To the creator within, I bow.

Precious Pranayama

104

Create

SPACE

for

Breath.

I AM

The lemurian quartz crystal encrusted cocoon cracks,
and I crawl out of the crevice of the chrysalis.

The celestial sunlight oozes up my citrine and lavender wings,
carrying precious prana with infinite exponential potential.

In the purity of the vibe and flow, I

LET GO.

The serpentine spiral slows to a sacred whisper
while the ALL releases me into
an intoxicating, energetic embrace.

My soul surrenders into an extravagant, eternal space
while the sweet taste of ambrosia awakens
my pineal and pituitary glands.
I receive knowing of the divine homecoming plan.
In the silence of the *now*, I hear
the silky, grounding voice of the

ONE

TRUE

I AM.

A voice sings—

*Give love without condition
like the great, central sun,
and you will realize everlasting perfection.*

Seed of Perfection

Bless your warrior spirit.

I found the will to fully embody my soul
in your reflection.

I watered the seed of perfection within.

It bloomed
and is now housed by this sensitive skin.

Each obstacle is a limit to transcend.
Every ending is an invitation to begin again.

This glorious realization
was found in the stream of cold showers
during delightful ambrosial hours.

Nanak's Japji
set me free.

Now,
I chant the divine's song eternally.

About the Author

Dijon Bowden is a multi-dimensional artist who believes in self-actualization as a means to inspire others to realize their own divinity. His meditation and yoga practice allow him to sustain a powerful connection to Source energy and channel visionary art.

Storytelling, music, poetry, photography, and filmmaking are vehicles he uses to share high vibrational healing energy.

SOULS of Society is a storytelling project that deepens compassion, empathy, and spiritual awareness in communities and has made millions of impressions online.

Indigo Keys is a musical project that produces cosmic soundscapes that are accompanied by cinematic visuals to create epic soulful experiences that speak to the human heart and soul.

Awakening Genius is a platform that exists to inspire the genius of visionary creatives all over the world, so we can build the New Earth.

From Infinity to Infinity is a multi-volume series of poetry chronicling the changing seasons of his journey.